Interview Success: A Step-by-Step Guide to Land Your Dream Job

By Evelina Raziel

Chapter 1: Mastering the Initial Call and Setting the Stage

Section 1: Responding to the Invitation

1.1 Prompt Acknowledgment:
Upon receiving the interview invitation, respond promptly. Express gratitude for the opportunity and your enthusiasm about the role.

1.2 Assessing Timing Challenges:
If the suggested interview time is inconvenient, approach the situation diplomatically. Politely express your commitment to the opportunity and inquire about the possibility of rescheduling.

1.3 Proposing Alternatives:
Instead of rejecting outright, suggest alternative dates and times. Showcase flexibility while ensuring that the rescheduled interview doesn't clash with existing commitments.

Section 2: Crafting Professional Communication
1.4 Maintaining a Positive Tone:
Craft a response that maintains professionalism and positivity. Use courteous language to convey your excitement about the upcoming interview.
1.5 Acknowledging Time Constraints:
Recognize the value of their time. Express understanding of the busy nature of the hiring process, showcasing your respect for their schedules.
1.6 Confirmation and Gratitude:
Once a new time is agreed upon, send a confirmation email. Reiterate your gratitude, express enthusiasm, and confirm interview details, including location and any specific instructions.

Section 3: Swift Preparations for Success

1.7 Immediate Research:

Start researching the company immediately. Familiarize yourself with its history, values, and recent developments. This knowledge will not only help you answer questions effectively but also demonstrate your genuine interest.

1.8 Understanding the Job Role:

Thoroughly analyze the job description. Identify key responsibilities and required skills, aligning your experiences with the job requirements to present yourself as a strong candidate.

1.9 Anticipating Common Questions:

Prepare for common interview questions related to experiences, strengths, weaknesses, and achievements. Develop concise, compelling responses that showcase your suitability for the role.

By effectively managing the initial call, communicating professionally, and swiftly initiating thorough preparation, you set the stage for a successful interview process. In the subsequent chapters, we'll delve deeper into strategies for interview success, covering topics ranging from resume crafting to mastering behavioral questions.

Scenario:
You receive a call from the company you applied to, inviting you for an interview. However, the proposed interview time is not convenient for you due to a prior commitment.

Response:
"Hello [Interviewer's Name],

Thank you so much for reaching out and providing me with the opportunity to interview for the [Job Title] position. I am genuinely excited about the possibility of joining **[Company Name]**.

I appreciate the proposed interview time, but unfortunately, I have a prior commitment scheduled during that period. I want to ensure I can dedicate my full attention to the interview process, as I believe this role is an excellent fit for my skills and experiences.

I understand the importance of your time, and I am more than willing to be flexible. Would it be possible to consider an alternative time for the interview? I am available [Proposed Date and Time], and I am confident that this adjustment will allow me to fully engage in the interview process.

Thank you again for this opportunity, and I look forward to the possibility of discussing my candidacy further.

Best regards,
[Your Full Name]
[Your Contact Information]

Chapter 2: Dressing for Success: A Comprehensive Guide to Appearance, Speech, and Knowledge

Section 1: The Power of First Impressions

2.1 Understanding the Significance:

In the competitive world of job interviews, first impressions matter. Your appearance is the initial indicator of your professionalism and commitment to the role. It sets the tone for the interview and can influence the interviewer's perception of your suitability for the position.

2.2 Researching the Company Culture:

Consider the company's culture when selecting your interview attire. For instance, if you're interviewing at a corporate law firm, a well-fitted suit would be appropriate. Conversely, if the company has a more relaxed startup culture, business casual attire might be suitable. Researching the company culture demonstrates your awareness and adaptability.

Section 2: Selecting the Right Outfit

2.3 Formal vs. Casual Attire:

For men, a tailored suit in a neutral color paired with a crisp shirt and tie is a classic choice. Women might opt for a professional business suit or a conservative dress. Ensure your clothing is clean and well-maintained. Grooming is equally crucial - tidy hair, minimal cologne or perfume, and well-groomed nails contribute to a polished look

2.4 Grooming and Personal Hygiene:

Attention to personal grooming is essential. Ensure your clothes are freshly pressed, your shoes are polished, and your overall appearance is neat. Maintain good personal hygiene, including clean hands and fresh breath, to create a positive and lasting impression.

2.5 Accessorizing Appropriately:

Limit accessories to a few key pieces that complement your outfit. A watch, tie pin, or modest jewelry can add a touch of sophistication. However, avoid anything too flashy or distracting.

Section 3: Preparing Your Speaking Skills

2.6 Practice Interview Responses:

Anticipate common interview questions and practice your responses. This not only sharpens your ability to articulate your thoughts but also helps you feel more confident during the actual interview. Consider mock interviews with a friend or family member for constructive feedback.

2.7 Work on Non-Verbal Communication:

Practice maintaining eye contact, delivering a firm handshake, and controlling your body language. These non-verbal cues convey confidence, enthusiasm, and engagement. Record yourself during practice sessions to identify areas for improvement.

2.8 Mastering the Elevator Pitch:

Craft a succinct and compelling elevator pitch that introduces you professionally. Highlight your key strengths, experiences, and what sets you apart from other candidates. This pitch serves as an excellent icebreaker and showcases your ability to communicate effectively.

Section 4: Enhancing Your Knowledge Base

2.9 Reviewing Industry and Company Information:
Stay informed about industry trends and recent developments related to the company. Knowing the company's background, values, and recent achievements allows you to tailor your responses and demonstrates your genuine interest in becoming part of their success.

2.10 Understanding the Role in Depth:
Thoroughly review the job description to understand the role's intricacies. This knowledge enables you to speak confidently about how your skills and experiences align with the specific requirements of the position. Be prepared to provide concrete examples of how your past achievements relate to the responsibilities outlined in the job description.

By paying attention to your appearance, refining your speaking skills, and enhancing your knowledge base, you'll confidently step into the interview room, leaving a lasting and positive impression on your potential employers. Chapter 3 will guide you through strategies for answering common interview questions and handling behavioral scenarios.

Chapter 3: Mastering Interview Questions and Navigating Behavioral Scenarios

Section 1: Strategies for Answering Common Interview Questions

3.1 Understanding the Purpose:

Interview questions serve as a window into your qualifications, experiences, and thought processes. Be prepared to articulate your responses clearly, emphasizing your strengths and aligning them with the requirements of the role.

3.2 Crafting Responses:

Practice answering common questions such as "Tell me about yourself," "Why should we hire you?" and "What are your strengths and weaknesses?" Develop concise, compelling responses that showcase your suitability for the position.

Scenario:

The interviewer opens with, "Tell me about yourself." You respond by providing a brief overview of your professional journey, highlighting key achievements and experiences relevant to the role.

3.3 Utilizing the STAR Method:

For behavioral questions requiring examples of past experiences, employ the STAR method (Situation, Task, Action, Result). This structured approach ensures your responses are well-organized and effectively demonstrate your capabilities.

Scenario:

When asked about a challenging project you managed, you describe the Situation, the Task at hand, the Actions you took, and the positive Result achieved.

Section 2: Handling Behavioral Scenarios

3.4 Anticipating and Preparing:

Identify potential behavioral questions related to teamwork, problem-solving, and conflict resolution. Reflect on your past experiences and be ready to discuss how you navigated challenges and contributed to positive outcomes.

Scenario:

The interviewer asks, "Can you provide an example of a time when you faced a conflict within a team and how you resolved it?" You respond by narrating a specific incident, emphasizing collaboration and the positive resolution achieved.

3.5 Showcasing Adaptability:

Be prepared to discuss situations where you had to adapt to change or handle ambiguity. Demonstrating your flexibility and ability to thrive in dynamic environments can set you apart from other candidates.

Scenario:

The interviewer inquires, "How do you handle unexpected challenges?" You respond by describing a situation where you successfully adapted to unexpected changes, showcasing your problem-solving skills.

Section 3: Follow-up Questions and Closing the Interview

3.6 Preparing Questions for the Interviewer:
Have thoughtful questions prepared for the interviewer. This demonstrates your genuine interest in the role and the company. Avoid asking questions that can be easily answered through basic research.

Scenario:
When asked if you have any questions, you inquire about the company's plans for future growth, showcasing your interest in long-term commitment.

3.7 Expressing Gratitude and Enthusiasm:
End the interview on a positive note by expressing gratitude for the opportunity. Reiterate your enthusiasm for the position and your eagerness to contribute to the team.

Scenario:
As the interview concludes, you thank the interviewer for their time, express your excitement about the potential opportunity, and convey your readiness to move forward in the hiring process.

By mastering common interview questions, navigating behavioral scenarios with confidence, and concluding the interview on a positive note, you position yourself as a well-prepared and capable candidate. In the upcoming chapters, we'll explore post-interview etiquette and negotiation strategies to further enhance your interview success.

Chapter 4: Advanced Interview Strategies - Navigating Complex Questions and Scenarios

Section 1: Handling Advanced Interview Questions

4.1 Navigating Challenging Questions:

Prepare for advanced questions that probe deeper into your decision-making process, leadership style, and strategic thinking. Anticipate inquiries such as "Can you provide an example of a time when you disagreed with a superior's decision, and how did you handle it?"

Scenario:

The interviewer asks about a time you disagreed with a superior's decision. You respond by describing the situation, your approach to resolving the disagreement professionally, and the positive outcomes.

4.2 Demonstrating Strategic Thinking:

Prepare to showcase your ability to think strategically. Expect questions like "How would you approach implementing a new initiative within our organization?" Craft responses that highlight your analytical skills and understanding of the company's goals.

Scenario:

The interviewer challenges you to implement a new initiative. You respond by outlining a strategic plan, emphasizing the alignment with the company's objectives, and addressing potential challenges.

Section 2: Navigating Hypothetical Scenarios

4.3 Handling Hypothetical Situations:

Be ready for questions that pose hypothetical scenarios relevant to the role. This tests your problem-solving abilities and how well you can apply your skills in different contexts.

Scenario:

The interviewer presents a hypothetical scenario related to a potential challenge in the role. You respond by breaking down the situation, proposing a strategic solution, and addressing potential outcomes.

4.4 Stress Testing Your Decision-Making:

Expect questions that stress-test your decision-making under pressure. The interviewer might present a scenario with conflicting priorities, and you'll need to articulate your thought process in resolving such challenges.

Scenario:

The interviewer presents a scenario where you have multiple urgent tasks. You respond by outlining your decision-making process, prioritizing tasks based on impact and deadlines, and ensuring effective communication.

Section 3: Demonstrating Industry Knowledge
4.5 Showcasing Industry Expertise:

Be prepared to demonstrate a deep understanding of your industry. Expect questions that assess your knowledge of current trends, challenges, and innovations.

Scenario:

The interviewer asks for your opinion on recent industry developments. You respond by discussing key trends, their implications, and how your skills align with staying ahead in the industry.

4.6 Linking Industry Insights to Company Goals:

Connect your industry knowledge to the goals of the specific company. Expect questions that inquire about your awareness of the company's position in the industry and how you can contribute to its success.

Scenario:

The interviewer asks how your understanding of industry trends can benefit the company. You respond by linking your insights to the company's goals, showcasing your strategic thinking.

Section 4: Handling Salary and Benefits Discussions

4.7 Navigating Salary Discussions:

Prepare for questions about your salary expectations. Research industry standards and be ready to negotiate effectively while keeping in mind the overall compensation package, including benefits.

Scenario:

The interviewer asks about your salary expectations. You respond by highlighting your research on industry standards, emphasizing the value you bring, and expressing openness to discuss a comprehensive compensation package.

By mastering advanced interview questions, navigating hypothetical scenarios with confidence, and effectively discussing salary and benefits, you position yourself as a candidate capable of handling the complexities of the role. In the next chapters, we'll explore post-interview etiquette and strategies for securing a successful job offer.

Chapter 5: Specialized Questions and Strategic Responses

Section 1: The "Tell Me About Yourself" Question

5.1 Personal Introduction:

How do you plan to introduce yourself concisely, highlighting your professional journey and key accomplishments?
What aspects of your background and experiences do you consider most relevant to the role?

Section 2: Explaining Employment Gaps and Departure from Previous Employment

5.2 Handling Employment Gaps:

If there's a gap in your employment history, how will you explain it in a way that demonstrates the value gained during that time?
How can you emphasize any relevant skills or experiences acquired during periods of unemployment?

5.3 Explaining Departure from a Previous Employer:

If you were at your previous job for a significant amount of time, how would you explain your departure without sounding negative about the company?
What positive aspects of your previous employment will you highlight, and how will you tactfully address any reasons for leaving?

Section 3: Addressing the "Why Are You Not Working There Anymore?" Question

5.4 Navigating the Question about Leaving Your Previous Job:

How will you frame your departure from your previous job positively?
What language will you use to discuss any challenges or changes in your previous role without sounding critical?

5.5 Emphasizing Career Growth:

How can you showcase that your decision to leave was driven by a desire for professional development and growth?
Are there specific skills or experiences you gained at your previous job that you can tie into your decision to move on?

Section 4: Demonstrating Continued Professional Development

5.6 Highlighting Professional Development:

How will you communicate your commitment to ongoing learning and development during periods of unemployment?
Can you discuss any certifications, courses, or projects you pursued to enhance your skills during breaks in employment?

5.7 Connecting Past Experiences to the New Role:

How will you link your previous long-term employment to the skills and experiences relevant to the new role?
Are there specific achievements or projects from your previous job that align closely with the requirements of the position you're interviewing for?

These questions and scenarios are designed to help you strategically approach common interview inquiries about your professional background, emphasizing positive aspects while addressing any potential concerns the interviewer might have. In the next chapter, we'll delve into post-interview etiquette and follow-up strategies.

Chapter 6: Post-Interview Etiquette and Effective Follow-Up Strategies

Section 1: Immediate Post-Interview Actions

6.1 Reflecting on the Interview:

What were your key takeaways from the interview, and how can you use them to your advantage?
Did you identify any areas where you can improve or provide additional information?

6.2 Sending a Thank-You Email:

How soon after the interview will you send a thank-you email to the interviewers?
What specific points from the interview will you express gratitude for in your thank-you note?

Section 2: Crafting a Thank-You Email

6.3 Personalizing Your Message:

How will you tailor your thank-you email to each interviewer, acknowledging specific topics discussed during the interview?
Can you include a memorable aspect from the conversation to make your message more personalized?

6.4 Reiterating Your Interest:

How will you restate your enthusiasm for the position and the company in your thank-you email?
Can you articulate why you believe you are the ideal candidate based on the interview discussion?

Section 3: Following Up on Additional Information

6.5 Providing Additional Information:

Were there any questions during the interview for which you promised to follow up with additional details?
How will you deliver this information in a way that reinforces your suitability for the role?

6.6 Reiterating Your Value Proposition:

How can you use follow-up communications to reinforce the unique value you bring to the position?
Are there specific examples or achievements you can highlight to further support your candidacy?

Section 4: Handling Multiple Interviews

6.7 Coordinating Follow-Ups with Multiple Interviewers:

If you interviewed multiple individuals, how will you coordinate follow-up emails to ensure consistency in your messaging?
Are there unique points from each interview that you should address in your follow-up messages?

Section 5: Timeline for Follow-Up

6.8 Setting a Follow-Up Timeline:

When do you plan to follow up after sending the initial thank-you email?
How frequently will you follow up without becoming overly persistent?

6.9 Adjusting Strategies Based on Company Practices:

Did the interviewer provide any information on the expected timeline for the hiring process?
How will you adjust your follow-up strategies based on the company's typical practices?
Section 6: Post-Interview Self-Reflection

6.10 Learning from the Experience:

What lessons can you extract from the interview experience, and how will you apply them to future opportunities?
Are there specific areas where you can enhance your interview skills based on this experience?
By implementing effective post-interview etiquette and thoughtful follow-up strategies, you not only demonstrate your continued interest in the position but also leave a positive and lasting impression on the interviewers. In the following chapters, we will explore negotiation techniques and preparation for potential job offers.

Chapter 7: Perfecting Your Speech and Voice for Confident Communication

Section 1: The Importance of Speech and Voice in Interviews

7.1 Recognizing the Impact:

How aware are you of the impact your speech and voice can have on interviewers?
Can you identify areas for improvement in your current speech and vocal patterns?

7.2 Conveying Confidence and Professionalism:

In what ways does a confident and professional speaking style contribute to a positive interview impression?
How might an effective use of voice enhance your overall communication during an interview?

Section 2: Techniques for Speech Improvement

7.3 Articulation Exercises:
Have you practiced articulation exercises to enhance the clarity of your speech?
Can you identify specific sounds or words that you find challenging to articulate clearly?

7.4 Varying Your Pitch and Tone:
How comfortable are you with varying your pitch and tone to convey different emotions or emphasis?
Can you experiment with different vocal tones to find a balance that feels authentic and professional?

Section 3: Voice Projection and Modulation

7.5 Developing Voice Projection:

Do you project your voice sufficiently to ensure clarity and audibility during an interview?
Are there situations where you may need to adjust your voice projection, such as in larger meeting rooms?

7.6 Modulating Your Voice:

How do you use voice modulation to convey enthusiasm, sincerity, or authority?
Can you practice modulating your voice to match the mood and content of different interview responses?
Section 4: Overcoming Nervousness and Speaking Anxiety

7.7 Breathing Techniques:

Have you explored breathing exercises to manage nerves and enhance your vocal control?
Can controlled breathing contribute to a calmer and more composed speaking demeanor?

7.8 Visualization for Confidence:

How might visualization techniques help you envision a successful interview, reducing anxiety in the process?
Can you visualize yourself speaking confidently and effectively during the actual interview?

Section 5: Continuous Practice and Feedback

7.9 Regular Speech Practice:

How often do you engage in deliberate practice sessions to refine your speech and vocal skills?
Can you integrate speech practice into your daily routine to make improvements over time?

7.10 Seeking Constructive Feedback:

Have you considered seeking feedback from peers, mentors, or communication professionals on your speech and voice?
How can constructive criticism contribute to ongoing improvement in your communication skills?
By proactively addressing speech and voice considerations, you enhance your ability to communicate with confidence and professionalism during interviews. Consistent practice, coupled with constructive feedback, will contribute to continuous improvement in your speaking skills. In the subsequent chapters, we will delve into strategies for negotiating job offers and successfully transitioning into a new role.

Chapter 8: Navigating Job Offers and Successful Negotiation

Section 1: Receiving and Evaluating a Job Offer

8.1 Understanding the Offer:

How thoroughly have you reviewed the job offer, including compensation, benefits, and other relevant details?
What aspects of the offer are particularly attractive to you, and where do you see room for negotiation?

8.2 Considering the Entire Package:

Beyond salary, what other components of the offer (benefits, work hours, flexibility) are important to your overall satisfaction?
Can you identify any potential concerns or areas where you'd like further clarification?

Section 2: Strategizing for Negotiation

8.3 Researching Market Standards:

How well-informed are you about industry standards and average compensation for your role?
Have you gathered data to support your negotiation points?

8.4 Defining Your Value Proposition:

What unique skills, experiences, or qualifications do you bring to the role that justifies negotiation for better terms?
Can you articulate a clear value proposition that aligns with the company's goals?

Section 3: Initiating the Negotiation Conversation

8.5 Expressing Enthusiasm and Gratitude:

How will you express your gratitude for the job offer while indicating your eagerness to discuss certain aspects?
What language will you use to maintain a positive and collaborative tone?

8.6 Choosing the Right Timing:

Have you considered when is the most appropriate time to initiate the negotiation conversation?
Are there external factors, such as the company's fiscal calendar, that may influence the timing?

Section 4: Effective Negotiation Techniques

8.7 Active Listening:

How can active listening contribute to a constructive negotiation dialogue?
Can you identify and address the concerns or priorities expressed by the employer during negotiations?

8.8 Win-Win Solutions:

How can you approach negotiation with a mindset of creating a win-win outcome for both parties?
Are there alternative benefits or terms you're willing to consider as part of the negotiation?

Section 5: Finalizing the Agreement

8.9 Confirming the Agreement in Writing:

Once an agreement is reached, how promptly will you confirm the details in writing?
What elements will you include in your written confirmation to avoid misunderstandings?

8.10 Maintaining Professionalism Throughout:

How will you ensure that the negotiation process maintains a professional and respectful tone?
Are there potential pitfalls or common negotiation mistakes you will actively avoid?
By approaching job offers and negotiations strategically, you position yourself for a successful transition into your new role. In the subsequent chapters, we will explore strategies for effective onboarding and making a positive impact in your early days at the new job.

Chapter 9: Seamless Onboarding and Early Success Strategies

Section 1: Preparing for the Onboarding Process

9.1 Understanding Company Policies:

How familiar are you with the company's policies and procedures?
Have you reviewed any pre-onboarding materials or documentation provided by the company?

9.2 Setting Up Practical Logistics:

Have you confirmed the details of your first day, including the start time, location, and any necessary documentation?
How will you handle logistics such as commuting, dress code, and initial introductions?

Section 2: Building Early Connections

9.3 Networking with Colleagues:

What strategies will you employ to connect with colleagues during your first days?
Are there specific individuals or teams you aim to meet to establish early working relationships?

9.4 Seeking Mentorship:

Have you identified potential mentors within the organization?
How will you approach individuals for mentorship in a way that demonstrates your eagerness to learn and grow?

Section 3: Absorbing Company Culture

9.5 Observing and Adapting:

How will you observe and adapt to the company's culture during the onboarding process?
Are there particular cultural nuances or values you should be aware of in your new workplace?

9.6 Understanding Team Dynamics:

How can you quickly grasp the dynamics of your new team?
Are there team-building activities or meetings scheduled during your onboarding period?

Section 4: Demonstrating Early Value

9.7 Taking Initiative:

In what ways can you take initiative and contribute meaningfully from the outset?
Have you identified any immediate opportunities to make a positive impact in your new role?

9.8 Communicating Effectively:

How will you ensure clear and open communication with your new team and superiors?
Are there regular check-ins or feedback sessions scheduled during the initial weeks?

Section 5: Seeking Feedback and Continuous Improvement

9.9 Requesting Feedback:

Have you proactively sought feedback on your performance and integration into the team?
How will you approach your superiors or colleagues for constructive feedback in a way that fosters growth?

9.10 Identifying Learning Opportunities:

Are there training sessions, workshops, or resources available to further develop your skills?
How will you identify and seize learning opportunities to enhance your capabilities in the early stages of your new role?

Section 6: Reflecting on Early Experiences

9.11 Reflecting on Early Challenges:

How will you navigate and learn from any challenges you encounter during the onboarding process?
Are there resources or support systems in place to help address potential hurdles?

9.12 Celebrating Early Wins:

How can you acknowledge and celebrate early successes in your new role?
Are there mechanisms in place for recognizing and sharing achievements within the team or organization?
By proactively engaging in the onboarding process and implementing strategies for early success, you set the foundation for a fulfilling and impactful journey in your new role.
In the following chapters, we will explore long-term career development and strategies for continuous growth within your organization.

Chapter 10: Long-Term Career Development and Continuous Growth

Section 1: Crafting a Long-Term Career Vision

10.1 Defining Career Goals:

What are your long-term career aspirations within the organization?
Have you articulated clear and achievable career goals that align with both personal and organizational objectives?

10.2 Aligning with Company Vision:

How can your individual career goals align with the company's long-term vision?
Are there opportunities for growth and advancement that resonate with both your ambitions and the organization's strategic direction?

Section 2: Building a Professional Development Plan

10.3 Identifying Skill Gaps:

What skills and competencies are essential for your desired career trajectory?
Have you conducted a self-assessment to identify areas for improvement and skill development?

10.4 Engaging in Ongoing Learning:

How will you stay updated on industry trends and new technologies relevant to your field?
Are there specific courses, certifications, or workshops you plan to undertake to enhance your skill set?

Section 3: Establishing a Mentorship Network

10.5 Building and Nurturing Relationships:

How will you continue to expand and nurture your professional
network within the organization?
Are there mentorship opportunities you can explore to gain
insights and guidance for career development?

10.6 Mentoring Others:

As you progress in your career, how can you contribute to the
growth of others through mentorship?
Have you considered taking on mentorship roles to share your
experiences and insights with junior colleagues?

Section 4: Embracing Leadership Opportunities

10.7 Developing Leadership Skills:

What steps will you take to develop and refine your leadership skills?
Are there leadership training programs, workshops, or opportunities for hands-on leadership experience within the organization?

10.8 Taking on Leadership Roles:

As you advance in your career, how can you actively seek and excel in leadership roles?
What leadership responsibilities align with your strengths and contribute to the organization's success?

Section 5: Navigating Career Transitions

10.9 Exploring New Opportunities:

How open are you to exploring different roles or departments within the organization?
Are there cross-functional opportunities that align with your skills and interests?

10.10 Adapting to Change:

How will you navigate and adapt to changes in the organizational structure or industry landscape?
Are there strategies for embracing change and leveraging it for personal and professional growth?

Section 6: Contributing to Organizational Success

10.11 Adding Value Continuously:

How can you consistently add value to your team and the organization?
Are there innovative ideas or projects you can initiate to contribute to the company's overall success?

10.12 Seeking Feedback and Iterating:

How will you actively seek feedback on your performance and areas for improvement?
Are you open to continuous iteration and refinement of your career development plan based on feedback and evolving organizational needs?
As you embark on your long-term career journey within the organization, these strategies for continuous growth, leadership development, and adaptability will contribute to a fulfilling and impactful professional life. Congratulations on completing this comprehensive guide to interview preparation, career success, and continuous development!

Bonus Section 1: Mastering Calmness with Deep Breathing Techniques

Interviews can be nerve-wracking, but the good news is that you have a powerful tool at your disposal to calm those nerves: deep breathing. Practicing deep breathing techniques before and during an interview can help you stay centered, focused, and present. Here are some simple yet effective techniques to incorporate into your pre-interview routine:

1. Diaphragmatic Breathing:

Find a quiet and comfortable place to sit or stand.
Place one hand on your chest and the other on your abdomen.
Inhale deeply through your nose, allowing your abdomen to expand.
Exhale slowly through your mouth, feeling your abdomen contract.
Repeat this process for several breaths, focusing on the rise and fall of your abdomen.

2. 4-7-8 Technique:
Inhale quietly through your nose to a mental count of four.
Hold your breath for a count of seven.
Exhale completely through your mouth to a count of eight.
This technique can help promote relaxation and ease tension.

3. Box Breathing:
Inhale for a count of four.
Hold your breath for a count of four.
Exhale for a count of four.
Pause for a count of four before inhaling again.
Repeat this pattern, creating a "box" with each breath cycle.

4. Visualization Breathing:

Close your eyes and picture a calm and serene place, like a beach or a peaceful forest.
Inhale slowly, imagining you are breathing in the tranquility of that place.
Exhale, releasing any tension or stress.
Repeat this process, allowing the visualization to bring a sense of calmness.

Tips for Using Deep Breathing Before an Interview:

Practice these techniques regularly, so they become familiar and easy to use.
Incorporate deep breathing into your pre-interview routine to help manage anxiety.
If possible, take a few minutes alone before the interview to focus on your breath.
During the interview, if you feel nervous, take a moment to silently engage in deep breathing to regain composure.
Remember, deep breathing is a simple but powerful tool to help you stay calm and composed during the interview process. It's a skill that, with practice, can become an essential part of your toolkit for success. Happy breathing, and best of luck with your interviews!

Bonus Section 2:

Here's a set of life coaching questions you can ask yourself when you're feeling scared or unprepared for an interview:

What Am I Afraid Of?

Identify the specific fears or anxieties you're experiencing. Are they related to the interview process, the questions you might be asked, or the fear of not being good enough?

What Can I Control in This Situation?

Focus on the aspects of the interview that you have control over. This might include your preparation, your mindset, and your responses during the interview.

What Have I Prepared For?

Remind yourself of the time and effort you've invested in preparing for the interview. List the key points and accomplishments you want to highlight.

What Are My Strengths?

Reflect on your strengths and positive qualities. What unique skills or experiences do you bring to the table? How can these strengths contribute to the role?

How Have I Overcome Challenges Before?

Recall instances in your life when you faced challenges and overcame them. What strategies did you use, and how can you apply those lessons to this situation?

What's the Worst-Case Scenario?

Consider the worst-case scenario realistically. Often, acknowledging and rationalizing these fears can help reduce their impact.

What's the Best-Case Scenario?

Envision a positive outcome. What would success look like in this interview? How would it feel to exceed your own expectations?

What Can I Learn from This Experience?

Shift your perspective to view the interview as a learning opportunity. What insights can you gain, regardless of the outcome? How can this experience contribute to your personal and professional growth?

Am I Being Too Hard on Myself?

Assess whether you're placing unrealistic expectations on yourself. Remember that it's okay not to be perfect, and mistakes can be valuable learning experiences.

What Self-Care Strategies Can I Implement?

Consider self-care practices that can help alleviate stress. This might include activities like deep breathing, meditation, or engaging in a favorite hobby before the interview.

Who Can Support Me?

Identify individuals in your support network whom you can reach out to for encouragement and guidance. Sometimes, a pep talk from a friend or mentor can make a significant difference.
What Would I Advise a Friend in This Situation?

Imagine a friend facing a similar challenge. What advice would you give them? Apply that same supportive and positive guidance to yourself.
Asking these questions can help you gain clarity, manage anxiety, and approach the interview with a more empowered and confident mindset. Remember, you've got this!